Working in Canadian Communities

JOBS IN SUBURBAN CANADA

TRUE NORTH

BY TODD KORTEMEIER

True North is published by Beech Street Books
27 Stewart Rd. Collingwood, ON Canada L9Y 4M7

www.beechstreetbooks.ca

Produced by Red Line Editorial

Photographs ©: Volodymyr Kyrylyuk/iStockphoto/Thinkstock, cover, 1; PhotoSerg/Shutterstock Images, 4–5; L Barnwell/Shutterstock Images, 6; SF photo/Shutterstock Images, 8–9; Kzenon/Shutterstock Images, 10; Firma V/Shutterstock Images, 12–13; Monkey Business Images/Shutterstock Images, 14–15, 16–17; wavebreakmedia/Shutterstock Images, 18–19; Red Line Editorial, 20–21

Editor: Heather C. Hudak
Designer: Laura Polzin

Library and Archives Canada Cataloguing in Publication

Kortemeier, Todd, 1986-, author
     Jobs in suburban Canada / by Todd Kortemeier.

(Working in Canadian communities)
Includes bibliographical references and index.
Issued in print and electronic formats.
ISBN 978-1-77308-027-7 (hardback).--ISBN 978-1-77308-055-0 (paperback).--
ISBN 978-1-77308-083-3 (pdf).--ISBN 978-1-77308-111-3 (html)

    1. Occupations--Canada--Juvenile literature. 2. Suburbs--Canada--Juvenile literature. 3. Suburban life--Canada--Juvenile literature. I. Title.

HF5382.5.C2K61 2016   j331.700971   C2016-903606-5
                                        C2016-903607-3

Printed in the United States of America
Mankato, MN
August 2016

TABLE OF CONTENTS

Chapter One

BUILDING BUSINESS

Canada is a huge country. It has big cities and small towns. Many Canadians live in an **urban** area. There are different communities within those areas. Cities develop outward. There's the **downtown** with big buildings. Then there are **neighbourhoods** where people live. At some point, the city stops growing outward. This is where the suburbs start.

Suburbs are communities that are close to a city. Some cities have many suburbs. Toronto is Canada's largest city. It is surrounded by big suburbs, such as Brampton and Markham. Edmonton is much smaller than Toronto. It still has suburbs. St. Albert and Spruce Grove are nearby.

Toronto has many suburbs.

Strip malls are common in suburbs across Canada.

Approximately two-thirds of Canadians live in suburbs. There have always been suburbs. But they became more common in the 1940s. That's when people started buying their own homes and cars. Both of those things are more common in suburbs. In cities people often rent apartments. They take buses or taxis or walk.

Suburbs are more spread out than cities. Most don't have a downtown or tall office buildings. They have more homes and smaller businesses. Most businesses serve the people living in suburbs. Restaurants, grocery stores, and retail stores are common sights. People in suburbs work in many types of jobs.

More than 14 million Canadians work in service jobs. Some of them work with food. They may wait tables or take your order at a restaurant. Others work as plumbers or painters.

Quarry Park in Calgary is a large suburb. It has enough office space for 20,000 workers. There are homes for 5,000 people. Seton is another suburb in Calgary. It is one of Canada's biggest suburbs. It has lots of office space. There are all sorts of small businesses and many kinds of jobs. Some people work as salespeople. They help people buy things. Other people in suburbs may work as dentists, hairdressers, butchers, or mechanics.

SUBURB TO CITY

Some Canadian suburbs have become full cities with suburbs of their own. One of these is Mississauga. It is southeast of Toronto. It was founded as a Toronto **township** in 1850. It grew to more than 100,000 people in the late 1960s. Then it became a city in 1974. Today it is one of Canada's largest cities. It has more than 700,000 people. It is home to some of Canada's largest companies. Many people there work in **finance**. Others have manufacturing jobs.

Chapter Two

MAKING THINGS

Canada makes a lot of products. Many Canadians work in manufacturing. There are lots of manufacturing companies in the suburbs. There is more space for a factory than in the city.

Cars are one of Canada's biggest manufacturing industries. There are five companies that build cars in Canada. More than 3,000 people work at the Brampton Assembly Plant outside of Toronto. Oakville is another Toronto suburb. Approximately 4,500 people work at a car factory there. A lot of them work on an **assembly line**. They build different parts of the cars. Some of them paint the body. Others put on the tires.

Approximately 180,000 people live in Oakville. It is located on the shores of Lake Ontario.

Some warehouse workers drive forklifts.

Many other products are made on an assembly line. Some workers drive vehicles called forklifts. They need a special licence to run them. These workers use forklifts to move heavy products around the factory. Other workers sell the products to people who need them.

It's not enough just to make products. Products need to be shipped to other parts of the country. Some workers put the products in boxes. Others load them onto trucks. Truck drivers take them to **warehouses**. These are huge buildings. Products are stored here until they can be sold.

Many suburbs have a lot of warehouses. In Calgary, warehouse workers send products to all of western Canada. People stock the products on shelves. They pack them up to send to stores and other businesses. Approximately 75,000 people in the Calgary area work in warehouses.

Warehouse workers find out where the products need to go. They make sure the products get to the right places. They may load them on a truck. Sometimes they send them to the airport.

Airports are often in suburbs, too. At airports, workers load products on planes. Some people work as mechanics. Others greet travellers.

IN THE AIR

Quebec is known for its **aerospace** industry. Nearly 37,000 Quebecois work in aerospace. Aerospace companies in Quebec make planes and helicopters. They also make flight **simulators** to train pilots.

Chapter Three

CONSTRUCTING CANADA

More than one million Canadians work in construction. Many work in suburbs. The suburbs are always growing. People need places to live. Businesses need offices. The suburbs are the site of many construction projects.

Abbotsford, British Columbia, is one of the fastest-growing suburbs in Canada. It is just outside Vancouver. It has more than 140,000 people. There are a lot of construction jobs. Approximately 11,000 people in Abbotsford work in construction. They build homes and businesses. They also help people fix up their homes. They may put a new roof on a house or paint the walls.

Sometimes construction workers build things in a shop. They take the parts to the work site to be put together.

A project needs many skilled workers. Architects design the building. Carpenters build the structure. They use saws and hammers to make the frame. Plumbers fit it with sinks and piping for water. Electricians make sure the building has power. Construction also creates jobs for **realtors**. They sell the homes once they are ready. They may rent out space to stores.

Many construction workers build houses in suburbs.

Chapter Four

HELPING OTHERS

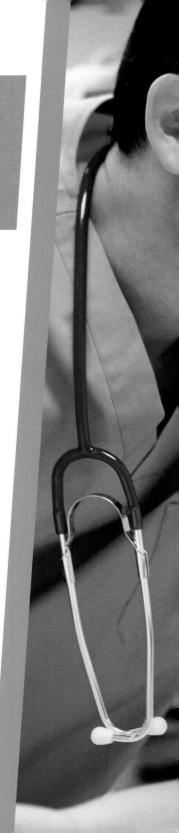

Most people in Canada work in the service industry. It has approximately 14 million workers. A lot of people who work in these jobs help others.

More people work in health care than any other industry in the country. It has more than two million jobs. Many health care workers help Canadians feel better. Some are doctors. Others are nurses. Psychiatrists help with mental health. Physical therapists help people recover from injuries.

Approximately 1.3 million Canadians work in education. In Edmonton most schools are in the city's core. As people move to the suburbs, new schools

Hundreds of thousands of Canadians work as nurses.

are being built. Some people help keep schools running. Cafeteria workers make sure everyone gets fed. Principals see to the day-to-day tasks. School bus drivers get kids to school safely.

Canada's suburbs are little cities on their own. They have all the services and housing their people need. More and more, Canada is becoming a suburban country.

INQUIRY QUESTIONS

What jobs are available in a suburb near you? What makes them different from jobs in other suburbs in your province, territory, or other parts of Canada?

There are more than 15,000 schools in Canada. Many are in the suburbs.

A SUBURBAN COMMUNITY

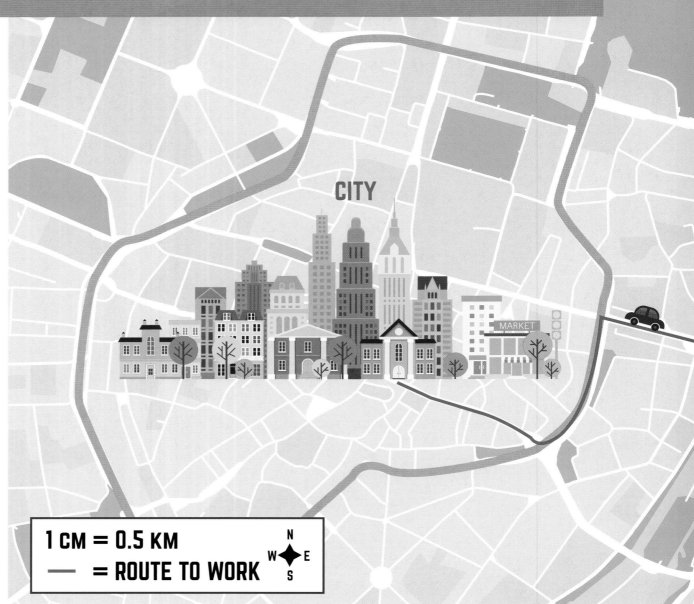

CITY

MARKET

1 CM = 0.5 KM

— = ROUTE TO WORK

N
W E
S

20

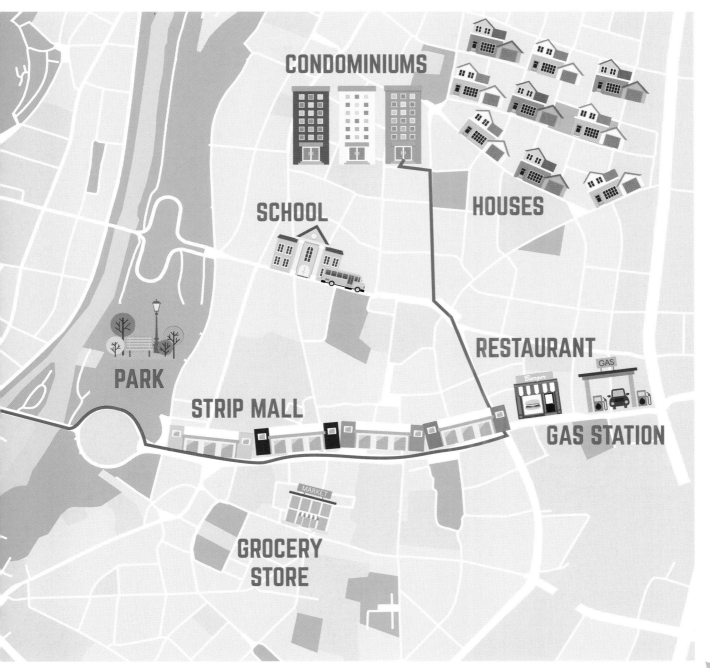

CONDOMINIUMS

HOUSES

SCHOOL

RESTAURANT

PARK

STRIP MALL

GAS STATION

GROCERY
STORE

21

GLOSSARY

AEROSPACE
an industry involved with airplanes and spacecraft

ASSEMBLY LINE
a lineup of machines and people in a factory who each build a part of an object

DOWNTOWN
the innermost part of a city with its tallest buildings

FINANCE
an industry concerned with managing money

MECHANICS
workers who fix machinery, such as car engines

NEIGHBOURHOODS
in a city or town, small areas where people live

REALTORS
people who sell houses

RETAIL
an industry based on selling products

SIMULATORS
machines that mimic what it is like to operate equipment or vehicles

TOWNSHIP
a type of small town

URBAN
an area that is not rural

WAREHOUSES
huge buildings with lots of interior space for storing products

TO LEARN MORE

BOOKS

Croza, Laurel. *From There to Here*. Toronto: Groundwood Books, 2014.

La Bella, Laura. *Getting a Job in Education*. New York: Rosen Publishing, 2016.

Marsico, Katie. *Suburb*. Ann Arbor, MI: Cherry Lake Publishing, 2014.

WEBSITES

CANADIAN GEOGRAPHIC KIDS!
www.canadiangeographic.ca/kids

KNOWITALL.ORG: EXPLORING CAREERS
http://media.knowitall.org/series/career-aisle-career-clusters

NATIONAL GEOGRAPHIC KIDS: CANADA
http://kids.nationalgeographic.com/explore/countries/canada/#canada-playing-hockey.jpg

INDEX

ABOUT THE AUTHOR

Todd Kortemeier is a journalist, an editor, and a children's book author. He has authored dozens of books for young people on a wide variety of topics.